The Socially Concerned Today

John Kenneth Galbraith

The
Socially Concerned Today

JOHN KENNETH GALBRAITH

Published in association with
Victoria University by
University of Toronto Press

© University of Toronto Press Incorporated 1998
Toronto Buffalo London
Printed in Canada

ISBN 0-8020-8161-4

Printed on acid-free paper

The Senator Keith Davey Lecture Series

Canadian Cataloguing in Publication Data

Galbraith, John Kenneth, 1908–
The socially concerned today

Includes bibliographical references.
ISBN 0-8020-8161-4

1. Economic history – 1990– .   2. Social policy.   I. Title
HC59.15.G35 1998   330.9′049   C97-932480-7

Credits: photo on p. ii by Jim Kalett;
photo on p. 52 courtesy Senator Keith Davey
photo on back cover: Reuters/Jim Young/Archive Photos

University of Toronto Press acknowledges the
financial assistance to its publishing program of the
Canada Council for the Arts and the
Ontario Arts Council.

Contents

CONCLUDING REMARKS

Note of Thanks

Afterword

BIOGRAPHICAL NOTES

Preface

DESPITE THE DRIVING WINDS and drifting snow of the worst storm of the winter of 1997, nearly one thousand people turned out to honour Senator Davey by applauding both his sterling career and his personal attributes, which have won him the friendship and respect of more than one prime minister and several generations of Canadians.

This volume represents the written record of an impressive moment, when town and gown (the general public, along with university professors and students) came together to acknowledge the impact of the vision of men such as Senator Keith Davey and Harvard professor and American presidential adviser John Kenneth Galbraith.

It is a great honour to introduce the essay that follows. Most of those who will read it have, like me, already had the privilege of reading some part of Galbraith's extensive writings. In my own case, I studied his books in a political economy course. I believe that the course was titled thus so that students could include it as part of a major in either political science or economics. I subsequently chose to major in literature – quite possibly because most of the authors we read did not write like Galbraith. Indeed, many economists deserve the epithet of George Bernard Shaw, who said that if one laid all the economists of the world end to end, one would not arrive at a conclusion. Obviously Shaw had not encountered an economist of Galbraith's stature!

Dr David Beach, dean of the University of Toronto's Faculty of Music, and his colleagues generously made the MacMillan Auditorium available for the first Davey lecture. Victoria University's student volunteers bravely guided guests through the blinding blizzard to an event that had been carefully planned, with the assistance of Victoria's faculty and staff. In addition, Cathy McCaulay and the staff of the Office of the President of the University of Toronto, as well as the staff of the University's Media Relations Office, were most generous in proffering their invaluable assistance.

Senator Jerry Grafstein, QC, had the original idea for this lecture series in honour of Senator Davey. He also provided the initiative and personal generosity that secured the endowment for this annual event. I would like to thank him, as well as each of the donors, most sincerely.

Through the generosity of the University of Toronto Press, this lecture series will make a lasting contribution to the communication of knowledge and ideas, helping us realize once again the central role and function of the university.

ROSEANN RUNTE
President
Victoria University

Introductory Remarks

Opening Remarks

SENATOR JERRY GRAFSTEIN, QC

THIS LECTURE REPRESENTS less a public dedication than a celebration of one man's lifelong passion. The Canadian constitution – the heart of our governance, that piece of paper that has so preoccupied, and continues to preoccupy in so many ways, so many of us – is silent, absolutely silent about two words that animate our public life. Those two words, which form the sinews and lifeblood of our constitution, are 'party politics.' They constitute as well the essence of Senator Keith Davey's enthusiasm.

Just as the late Northrop Frye, that great exemplar of Victoria University, spent his life here, exploring the mysterious canons and hidden patterns buried in literature, so this lecture celebrates the life and work of Keith Davey. Davey spent practically every waking hour from his student days at Victoria in the 1940s (except time diverted to family and sports) on one, all-encompassing mania. His goal was first to chart and then to forge those invisible and not-so-invisible links of 'party politics.' To be even more precise, he devoted his time to the politics of one party! I can personally attest to the veracity of this statement.

Last year Senator Davey surprised his friends at his birthday party with the announcement that he was retiring from public life, after almost four decades of unblemished and honourable participation. However, he made it emphatically clear that he did not intend to put aside his interests in politics and party politics. In view of his unflagging zeal, there could be no more fitting or lively honour to bestow on him than to create the annual Senator Keith Davey Lecture in Canadian Politics at Victoria University.

Last June, hundreds of friends – allies and adversaries alike – gathered in Ottawa to hold dinner in honour of Keith Davey and Allan J.

MacEachen, who were both retiring from the Upper House. A tribute committee coordinated a successful drive to raise the funds to endow this lecture, which was announced on that auspicious evening. I would like to take this opportunity to thank all of the generous contributors who made this annual event possible. I would like also to thank the members of the organizing committee for their creativity and hard work, which made this remarkable occasion possible.

The inauguration of the series by Professor John Kenneth Galbraith is most auspicious indeed. Dr Galbraith has, throughout his astonishing and prolific career, never failed to give liberalism a good name. Hailing from southwestern Ontario, he understands the Canadian context and our plans and concerns for social programs. Since I was born in London, Ontario, just a few miles from Elgin County, where our guest lecturer was born, and since I find myself in such agreement with his ideas, I can only conclude that there must be a special quality in the air in southern Ontario!

I would like to conclude with a personal word to Keith Davey. Should you ever change your mind and wish to come out of retirement, please give me a call!

Thank you, Victoria University; thank you, ladies and gentlemen; thank you, Dorothy and Keith.

Introduction

J. ROBERT S. PRICHARD
President
University of Toronto

YOUR HONOUR, CHANCELLOR WOLFE, Prime Minister Trudeau, Senator Davey, honoured guests, colleagues, ladies and gentlemen. It is a singular pleasure for me as president of the University of Toronto to have the opportunity to introduce the inaugural Senator Keith Davey lecturer, one of the finest scholars in any discipline that Canada and, in particular, this province have ever produced: Professor John Kenneth Galbraith.

Paul M. Warburg Professor of Economics Emeritus at Harvard University, Professor Galbraith hardly needs any introduction. He is probably the best-known economist on the planet. His talent in his field is well and widely recognized in academe. He has been a major presence at California, Princeton, and since 1948 at Harvard. Moreover, Professor Galbraith's mastery of the written word has allowed him to share his cogent observations on the economic and social patterns of our age with an unprecedented readership through his more than twenty-five books.

Even those who have not read *The Affluent Society*, *The New Industrial State*, or, most recently, *The Good Society* have heard of them, and most certainly been touched by their influence. Others know our lecturer for his reflective study of his own Ontario and Scottish roots in *The Scotch* or from his novels, *The Triumph* and *A Tenured Professor*. In the *Affluent Society* he told us that 'the shortcomings of economics are not original error but uncorrected obsolescence.' And he has devoted his rich career to trying to correct that obsolescence. He remains a vital, stimulating, and provocative presence, advancing his cause.

Professor Galbraith was born at Iona Station, Ontario, on 15 October 1908. He earned a bachelor of science degree from the University of Toronto when he graduated from the

Ontario Agricultural College in Guelph in 1931. He returned in 1961 to receive an honorary doctorate of laws from the University of Toronto, long after completing his master's and PhD degrees at Berkeley. And it is some evidence of his extraordinary standing that he has received over forty-four additional hononary degrees.

An advocate of Keynesian and post-Keynesian economics, Dr Galbraith honed his academic and professional skills in the midst of the Great Depression and Franklin D. Roosevelt's New Deal. A naturalized American citizen since 1937, and a long-time member of the Democratic party, he distinguished himself in U.S. public service, first during the Second World War as deputy administrator in the Office of Price Administration under President Roosevelt. His wartime service earned him the Medal of Freedom in 1946. He subsequently served a succession of Democratic presidential candidates and presidents, including Adlai Stevenson. John Kennedy – whom he also served as U.S. ambassador to India from 1961 to 1963 – and Lyndon Johnson. His wisdom and good counsel continue to be sought by decision makers and heads of state around the world.

In a career marked by remarkable longevity and productivity, Professor Galbraith has held many of the most respected positions to which a scholar can aspire, including chair of the American Academy of Arts and Letters for Literature, president of the combined American Academy and Institute of Arts and Letters, and president of the American Economic Association.

There is no one alive more appropriate to give the inaugural Davey Lecture than John Kenneth Galbraith. There is no one more clearly identified with liberalism in Canada than Senator Davey, and no more prominent and important liberal in the United States than Professor Galbraith. No one writes more passionately, persuasively, or productively on liberalism than Dr Galbraith; and no one promotes liberalism more passionately or persuasively in Canada than Senator Davey. John Kenneth Galbraith is the only economist alive who makes people laugh; and it has been Keith Davey more than anyone else who has made membership in the Liberal party of Canada fun.

Galbraith and Davey. Two great sons of the University of Toronto; liberals in word and deed; believers in the activist state; two men who have left very large marks in their chosen callings.

It is with great pleasure that I introduce to you Professor John Kenneth Galbraith.

The Inaugural Senator Keith Davey Lecture

The Socially Concerned Today

JOHN KENNETH GALBRAITH
Paul M. Warburg
Professor of Economics Emeritus
Harvard University

THERE HAS LONG HERE IN CANADA been a well-justified suspicion of onetime Canadians who come back to their parent country to offer advice. There is the question: If so enlightened and so disposed to offer guidance, why did they not just stay here? This is a risk that I will not run today. It is, instead, my pleasure to join in the celebration of Keith Davey, a most distinguished and effective political leader,

The Inaugural Senator Keith Davey Lecture in Politics, Victoria University, delivered in the MacMillan Auditorium, Faculty of Music, University of Toronto, at 4 p.m., Thursday 9 January 1997.

whose views I strongly applaud. He belongs with Mike Pearson and Pierre Trudeau as one of the truly enlightened and effective Canadian leaders of the past half-century. You honour me in allowing me to honour him.

I am also pleased to be back at what, by generous definition, is my alma mater. (In my day, now some seventy years ago, we agriculturalists at Guelph did consider ourselves somewhat a group apart – a view that was, I believe, shared here in Toronto.)

My comments on this happy occasion today apply, or are meant to apply, to all of the economically advanced world. I do not single out Canada (or even Ontario) for special attention. My concern is the political position and goals of the socially concerned, wherever they live and however they are designated – Socialists in France and other lands, Social Democrats in Germany, the Labour party in Britain, liberals in the United States, and the socially concerned, however denoted, here in Canada. I will avoid any political designation.

Where and for what in these socially complex and sometimes politically retrograde times do, should, the socially concerned take their stand? Some of the special motivation for these comments comes, I cannot doubt, from recent developments in the United States and Canada. In the United States, the war against the poor having now been won, there is a special urgency as regards some of the matters I will cover. This, I judge, is also true here in Canada, and to this I will respond. What are the fundamentals of the position of those I have called the socially concerned?

Common to all countries now is the basic market system for the production of goods and services – the word 'capitalism,' we must note, is no longer politically quite correct. The market system produces goods and services in the favoured countries of the world in manifest abundance – an abundance so great that large sums of money must now be spent to cultivate the wants it then supplies. We, the socially concerned, do not accept that this performance is without flaw; that I will sufficiently urge. But in the world as it exists, there is clearly no plausible alternative. The age of presumed choice between alternative economic systems is over. The present preoccupation with consumer satisfaction, original and contrived, may be regretted. There are serious environmental issues in the world. Problems of sustainable resource supply will be ever more pressing in the future. (When I met the Dalai Lama a few months ago, he asked me what the world would be like were everyone possessed of, and driving, an automobile.) There is also the strong political voice that the market system accords those who own or manage its productive apparatus. From this economic position and their money derive political influence and power. But, to repeat, the system itself we accept; even the British Labour party, long the custodian of a richly endowed dissent, has now rendered such acceptance fully. So too have most in Canada and, one cannot doubt, across the border.

Let us also be fully aware of another circumstance: the survival and acceptance of the modern market system were, in large measure, the accomplishment of the socially concerned. It would not have so survived had it not been for our successful civilizing efforts. Capitalism in its original form was an insufferably cruel thing. Only with trade unions, the protection of workers and workers' rights, pensions for the old, compensation for the unemployed, public health care, lower-cost housing, a safety net, however imperfect, for the unfortunate and the deprived, and public action to mitigate capitalism's commitment to boom and slump did the market system become socially and politically acceptable. Let us not be reticent: we, the socially concerned, are the custodians of the political tradition and action that saved classical capitalism from itself. We are frequently told to give credit where credit is due. Let us accept it when it is ours.

Let us also note that this salvation was accomplished over the strong, often-vehement opposition of those so saved. That opposition remains to this day. The individuals and economic institutions most in the debt of both economic advance and social tranquillity are those that, with the money and voice just mentioned, most oppose, seek most strongly to reverse, the action that serves those ends. Nothing on the political right is so certain as its opposition to what advances its own deeper, more durable interest.

In recent years there has been a current of thought (or what is so described) which holds that all possible economic activity should be returned to the market. The market system having been accepted, it must now be universal; privatization is a public faith. This, needless to say, we reject. The question of the private versus the public role should not be decided on abstract, theoretical grounds; the decision depends rather on the merits of the particular case. Conservatives need to be warned (as we must also warn ourselves) that ideology can be a heavy blanket over thought. Our commitment must always be to thought.

Thought must also guide action on the continuing flaws, inequities, and cruelties in the market system, of which I shall outline three, and on the requisite social action. There is, perhaps most notably, the very evident fact that the market is unreliable in its performance – that it moves from good times to bad, from boom to bust. In this process it brings deprivation and despair to the most vulnerable of its willing and unwilling participants. The only valid design is for an economy of steady well-being. This requires strong, intelligent public intervention to temper the speculative boom and to ensure against hardship and deprivation in the depressive aftermath. This is a matter of high current relevance. We are currently witnessing – and, in the frequent case, rejoicing in – a stock market boom, a bubble, for which we may be reasonably sure there will be an unpleasant day of reckoning.

There is no novelty as to what is required: the relevant action is the product of the best in economic thought over the past century. We must not live in fear of strong, productive economic performance, but we must have well in mind the danger of excess. In good times the public budget – taxes and expenditures – must be a restraining force. So also action against mergers and acquisitions and other manifestations of adverse, sometimes insane, corporate behaviour. Monetary restraint, which entails higher interest rates, is in order, a matter on which conservatives are more than adequately agreeable. And there must also be general public recognition that the system is, by its nature, given to such speculative excess. There is usually merit, and perhaps possible caution, in recognizing the inevitable. So there would be now.

In recession and against unemployment the course of action is better defined. There must be low interest rates to encourage borrowing for investment, an action also accepted by conservatives, who always see in the detached, hygienic, financially oriented or controlled activities of a central bank a substitute for more effective anti-depressive policy. There must also be further and effective fiscal measures to increase employment. The social loss and human distress of unemployment must be directly addressed. This means alternative public employment in recession or depression; the social waste of idleness cannot be accepted.

This is the broad Keynesian design. The main current of modern conservatism holds that it has gone out of fashion. Fashion, let us agrees, should not be a controlling force in economic policy. There is no substitute in recession for a policy of publicly insured employment, with resulting economic support and growth. That must continue to be the good of the socially concerned.

One large and influential sector of alleged thought now accepts recurrent stagnation and recession and, indeed, greatly prefers them to public action to counter their effect. In this view, unemployment is a necessary preventative against inflation. We cannot be casual about inflation; as necessary, it must be restrained. As I have noted, we urge monetary action and fiscal restraint in inflation-prone times. Where negotiated wage and price restraints are relevant, we are willing to urge them. But in the future, as in the past, we must accept a modest increase in prices as a condition for steady economic growth. We, the socially concerned, do not seek the euthanasia of the rentier class, but we do not accept that an all-pervasive, malignant fear of inflation should arrest all economic progress.

We accept the need for fiscal responsibility. This, however, does not mean an annually balanced budget; in the United States at the moment that aim is a major weapon in the larger attack on the poor. Borrowing for the with enhanced future return is legitimate for government, as it is for corporations and individuals. The valid test is that increased debt should be in keeping with increased ability to pay. I do not speak with confidence as to Canada, but that broadly is the present situation across the border.

A reliably growing economy begins, but it by no means ends, the agenda of the socially concerned. There is another very specific flaw in the market system against which we must rally political strength and action. The market system distributes income in a highly unequal fashion. The United States, it is now clear, exercises an adverse world leadership in this regard. Strong and effective trade union organization, a humane minimum wage, social security, and good medical care are a recognized part of the answer. On this we agree. So also a stoutly progressive income tax. Few exercises in social argument are made so obviously in defence of financial self-interest as those brought forward by the rich against their taxes. It always boils down to the slightly improbable case that the rich are not working because they have too little income, the poor because they have too much. Or, calling on my rural Ontario origins in Elgin County, to what may be called the horse-and-sparrow theory – this holds that if you feed the horse enough oats, some will pass through to the road for the sparrows. Perhaps, who knows? Nothing so contributes to energy and initiative in the modern economy as a struggle to sustain and enhance after-tax income, but this is a point I do not press.

We, the socially concerned, do not seek equality in income distribution. People differ in ability and aspiration in the pursuit of both financial reward and gain. There is also the role of initiative, luck, and avarice. This must be accepted. There can be no retreat, however, from the goal of a socially defensible distribution of income. This, to repeat, the tax system must continue to address. We must expect, and we need not respond to, screams of anguish from the very rich. Our mission reflects the old Pulitzer purpose – to comfort the afflicted and afflict the comfortable.

There must also be firm recognition of yet another major flaw of the market system. That is its allocation of income as between public and private services and functions. In the United States, private television is richly financed; urban public schools are badly starved. Private dwellings are clean, tolerable, and pleasant; public housing and public streets are filthy. Libraries, public recreational facilities, basic social services – all needed more by the poor than by the rich – are seen as a burden. The private living standard, in contrast, is good, sacrosanct. This anomaly we do not tolerate.

A few months ago I was in California for a commencement address at Berkeley, the other of the two universities of my youth to which I am deeply grateful. There one heard of little else except the budget cuts the university was enduring. This in a rich state, replete with consumer goods and resources in the billions for morally depraved television productions. It makes no sense at all.

We cannot tolerate such deviant error as regards education. High professional competence, adequate, indeed generous, financing, and wise, effective discipline must make education available to all. The justification is not alone that a well-educated labour force enhances economic productivity, the regrettable present case. It is, rather, that good education enhances, enriches, the enjoyment of life. That is its true justification.

There must be, most of all, an effective safety net – individual and family support – for those who live on the lower edges of the system or below. This is humanely essential. It is also necessary for human freedom. Nothing sets such stern limits on the liberty of the citizen as a total absence of money.

In the United States, as I have said, there has just been a two-year attack on the welfare system – in plain language, the war of the affluent against the poor. Other countries have had a similar manifestation, not excluding this favoured land. In this conflict there is no question as to where we, the socially concerned, must stand. There must be strong support of the social measures that protect the poorest of our people. A rich society can do no less.

We should also be aware of one important cause of this attack on public services and on the safety net for the poor. It is another of the accomplishments of the socially concerned. Over the years we brought social programs into being – health care, social security, measures for a stronger, more effectively working economy, and much else. In doing so, we made many people secure in their well-being and in consequence, as might be expected, more conservative in their public attitudes and expression. They now see help to the less fortunate as a threat to their own often ample and increasing incomes.

Let us always be aware that this was our political achievement. In creating the modern, more socially functional, more compassionate society, we created at the same time the culture of personal contentment. But let us not be sorry. We also, as I have said, saved the system.

I turn finally to the larger international scene. A closer association between the major economic powers is a fact of our times. Trade, finance, the international corporation, travel, technology, and cultural activity have all had this effect. In contrast with the two wars that so darkened the first half of the twentieth century, not least here in Canada, this is a strongly favourable development, for which there can be no regret. Unrestrained nationalism has a cruel and depressing history. There are, however, conditions on which we must insist before embracing a policy of internationalism.

The move towards closer association cannot be at cost to the welfare systems of the participating states. These must be protected, and this effort requires joint international action. There must be effective coordination of social welfare policy, and of the more general and controlling fiscal and monetary policy. It is on these – not, as now, on a socially barren trade policy – that presidents and prime ministers increasingly must concentrate (and agree) when they meet. There is no case for a narrow commitment to the nation-state. But neither can there be one to a mindless internationalism that sacrifices the social gains of the century just past and those that we still need. Internationalism will proceed; it must, however, do so hand in hand with both the coordination and the protection of national social and welfare policy.

There is another international obligation that the fortunate countries must recognize: concern for human well-being does not stop at national frontiers. It must extend on to the poor of the planet; hunger, disease, and death are equally a source of human suffering wherever they are experienced. On this all civilized peoples must agree.

The worst of suffering now comes from internal disorder and conflict. The people of the fortunate countries, on the whole, live peacefully together. This is one of the rewards of well-being. Life in this world is preferred to an early transfer to the next. It is the poor, with little to lose and with higher expectations in the next world, who devastate and destroy each other. There must, accordingly, be a reliable commitment by the fortunate countries to end conflict, bring order when and where this is humanely essential. I do not see this as the special responsibility of any one country, not particularly the United States. It must be effective and well-financed task of the United Nations. The claims of national sovereignty do not, must not, permit the mass slaughter of the poorest of the poor by the poor.

Beyond this, there must be an absolute obligation for the rich countries to give help. This is a matter with which I have long been concerned; we must not yield to the argument that because people are still poor, the earlier help has been ineffective. In the first stages of development effort we were, indeed, too eager to transport the heavy industrial furniture of the developed lands – steel mills, electric generators, airports – to the new countries. Human investment – that in health and education – we have now come to recognize, is of higher urgency. Over the world, let us be clear: there is no literate population that is poor; no illiterate population that is other than poor.

Let us also be aware – a matter not earlier understood – that what is possible and right in the way of social and economic action in the favoured countries cannot be transferred without thought to the poor. This, too, has been attempted in the past. Governments of sadly limited competence were given social and economic tasks that were beyond their capacity for honest, effective action. All things, including social policy, must be in keeping with the larger, controlling social and political environment. The early roles of government and of the relatively unhindered agricultural and urban economy of the now-advanced countries were appropriate one to the other. Economic life and the social role of the state must similarly be in accord in the new nations. Failure to recognize this necessity was a serious error of the socially concerned as they first approached the problem of economic development.

I come to the end of these remarks. Let our mood be good. The social attitude and action I have urged today were not the cerebral invention of the politically inclined. We, the socially concerned, were not that resourceful, that innovative. Change was given to us by history – by the requirements and the opportunities of a highly developed economic and social structure.

The elementary agrarian economy of past times did not suffer unemployment. There was always work on a farm; the young then cared for the old. Health care was not vitally important; before the great modern advances in medicine and surgery, the physician had little to sell. The choice between illness and health, death and life, was not controlled by ability to pay. It was urbanization that made necessary a great range of public services, including a comprehensive and compassionate structure of welfare support. (The latter was certainly not essential in metropolitan Iona Station, population twenty-three, near where I was born.)

Those who would reverse social action or even allow it to stagnate in the present are not in conflict with the socially concerned; they are at odds with the great force of history. We can have a measure of sympathy for them – for those who oppose us. We, not they, are in step with history. But we should also be aware of our own role. It was one not of invention but of accommodation. The world and its commitment to change being as they are, there will be continuing need for adjustment. Our task – that of all who are in compassionate step with history – is never over. While we resist those who seek to arrest or reverse such accommodation, we must be in step with further change.

So I bring this discourse to an end – this tribute to Senator Davey, a leader who, I venture to believe, is broadly in sympathy with what I have urged today. The difference is that I have urged, while he has acted.

I end also with an affirmation of my pleasure in being back in what I am still privileged to call my homeland. I thank my audience and my readers for their patient and tolerant attention to my ideas, my ideals, and my enduring idealism.

Concluding Remarks

Note of Thanks

JOHN MEISEL
Emeritus Professor
Queen's University

ANYONE CALLED ON TO FOLLOW John Kenneth Galbraith at a podium confronts two major obstacles. The first arises from the fact that a person of normal size stands about a foot below him and consequently is not anywhere within shouting distance of the microphone. The organizers of today's event helpfully foresaw this problem and provided a stoop on which we shorter – and lesser – mortals can strive to reach our guest's dizzying height. And it is, of course, much more difficult to equal the *intellectual* altitude invariably attained by Professor Galbraith, and no one has, alas, offered to give me a leg up in that department.

Among the remarkable bundle of his talents, the awesome excellence of his mind stands out. But almost equally striking is his extraordinary ability to write and speak in a manner that makes even his most difficult ideas accessible to everyone. The lucidity, seductive wry humour, and felicity of expression, on top of the substance of what he says, make of Professor Galbraith one of the titans of our age.

In a preface to one of his collections of essays, Arthur Koestler (who gave us almost as many books as John Kenneth Galbraith) ascribes to Albert Einstein the advice I remember as follows: 'If you deal with complex subjects, you had better leave elegance to your tailor.' Well, the gracefulness of expression in today's lecture shows that even Einstein could get it wrong.

At a recent conference Ed Broadbent referred to Professor Galbraith as 'one of Canada's best exports to the United States.' His lecture this afternoon has shown us why. What we have just experienced is not only a stimulating, aesthetic pleasure, but also an opportunity to receive a magnificent charter to guide the socially concerned towards more reasonable, caring, and humane policies than those currently pursued by our governments.

Professor Galbraith, you have eloquently exposed grievous flaws in the current social, economic, and political landscape, and you have provided guidance towards paths now sadly ignored or neglected by those responsible for the public weal. You have provided a badly needed voice, and you did it without even once mentioning Meech Lake or Charlottetown. We thank you for a truly splendid inauguration of the Keith Davey Lecture.

Afterword

SENATOR KEITH DAVEY

THERE SIMPLY COULD not have been a more thoughtful and generous gift than the establishment of this lecture series at my alma mater, Victoria University. I would like to express my gratitude to all the people who made this first lecture, the series, and this publication possible. Those who contributed to the endowment of this series should be applauded warmly for their generosity.

I would like to thank especially Senator Jerry Grafstein for his initiative and effort. This project was truly his brainchild and the result of his work. I am deeply grateful to him for all he has done to create this lecture series and to endow it so that it will make a lasting contribution to our knowledge of politics in Canada.

Finally, I am grateful to the University of Toronto Press; to Victoria University, Roseann Runte, president; and to the members of the organizing committee, which included Larry Davies, Martha Drake, Diane Dubé, Paul Fox, Sarah Gray, Jock Galloway, Bill Harnum, Roger Hutchinson, Brian Merrilees, and Robert Vipond.

Biographical Notes

John Kenneth Galbraith

JOHN KENNETH GALBRAITH is Paul M. Warburg Professor of Economics Emeritus at
Harvard University. He is internationally
known for his development of Keynesian and
post-Keynesian economics and the economics
of the modern large firm, as well as for his writing and his active involvement in American
politics.

Professor Galbraith was born on 15 October
1908 at Iona Station, Elgin County, Ontario.
He earned his BS degree from the University
of Toronto (Ontario Agricultural College) in
1931 and an MS (1933) and a PhD (1934) from
the University of California at Berkeley. He

became a U.S. citizen in 1937 and taught at both California and Princeton before going to Harvard permanently in 1948. He has received some forty-five honorary degrees from universities worldwide, including Harvard, Oxford, Paris, Moscow State, and Toronto.

Professor Galbraith has had a distinguished career in American and international politics. A Democrat, he served as President John F. Kennedy's ambassador to India from 1961 to 1963. Under President Franklin D. Roosevelt, Galbraith was deputy administrator in the early 1940s in the Office of Price Administration, where he organized and administered the wartime system of price controls. He also served as director of the U.S. Strategic Bombing Survey in 1945. For his public service, Galbraith was awarded the Medal of Freedom in 1946.

Professor Galbraith campaigned with Adlai Stevenson in 1952 and 1956, was an economic adviser to Senator John F. Kennedy during the 1960 presidential race, and, as chair of Americans for Democratic Action, supported Senator Eugene McCarthy's bid for the presidency, helping to put his name in nomination at the Democratic convention in 1968. He was an early and continuing opponent of the war in Vietnam.

Professor Galbraith, known for his lucid, persuasive writing style, has published many books and articles. The *Affluent Society* (1958), for which he won the Tamiment Book Award and the Sidney Hillman Award, challenged the myth of the U.S. economy's reliance on the gross national product for its social stability, positing instead that consumers' taste for luxury goods dictated the economy's focus, at the expense of the common welfare. The *New Industrial State* (1967) and *Economics and the Public Purpose* (1973) continued the examination of this thesis, to critical and popular acclaim.

Other works that have garnered Professor Galbraith an international audience include *American Capitalism* (1952), *The Great Crash* (1955), *Economics and the Art of Controversy* (1955), *The Liberal Hour* (1960), *The Scotch* (1964), best-selling novel *The Triumph* (1968), *Ambassador's Journal* (1969), *A China Passage* (1973), *Money: Whence It Came, Where It Went* (1975), *The Age of Uncertainty* (1977), *Almost Everyone's Guide to Economics* (1979), *The Nature of Mass Poverty* (1979), *A Life in Our Times* (1981), *The Voice of the Poor* (1983), *The Anatomy of Power* (1983), *A View from the*

Stands (1986), *Economics in Perspective* (1987), *Capitalism, Communism and Coexistence* (with Stanislav Menshikov, 1988), a second novel, *A Tenured Professor* (1990), *The Culture of Contentment* (1992), and *A Journey through Economic Time* (1994). *The Good Society* was published in April 1996. Galbraith has also written on Indian art, modern urban planning and design, civil rights, and American foreign policy. He was an editor of *Fortune* from 1943 to 1948 and has published in economic journals and in popular periodicals such as the *New York Review of Books*, the *New Yorker*, and the *New York Times Magazine*.

He has been president of the American Economic Association, a fellow of Trinity College, Cambridge (of which he is now an honorary fellow), a visiting fellow at All Souls College, Oxford, and an honorary professor at the University of Geneva's Graduate Institute of Advanced International Studies. He is a member of the American Academy of Arts and Sciences and has been an honorary foreign member of the Academy of Sciences of the U.S.S.R. and now that of Russia. In 1982 he was elected to the fifty-member American Academy of Arts and Letters for Literature, occupying the chair once held by Archibald MacLeish. From 1984 to 1987 he was president of the combined American Academy and Institute of Arts and Letters. In November 1997 he was inducted as an honorary Officer of the Order of Canada.

Professor Galbraith is married to the former Catherine Atwater, and they are the parents of three sons. Professor and Mrs Galbraith reside in Cambridge, Massachusetts, during the academic year and in Newfane, Vermont, in the summer.

Senator Keith Davey

B ORN IN TORONTO on 21 April 1926, the same day as Princess (now Queen) Elizabeth in Britain, Keith Davey was the son of Charles 'Scotty' Minto Davey and Grace Viola Curtis. He attended North Toronto Collegiate Institute, graduating in 1946 and going on to Victoria University, where he received a BA in 1949. He was an excellent student and president of the student council to boot, though in his typically self-deprecating fashion, he recalls that at one point his grades were so poor that he had to surrender the Senior Stick. His humility prevented him from noting that the prized honour was awarded to the student with the

Senator Keith Davey

highest grades who also participated actively in campus life.

Following his graduation from university and a brief stint at the Faculty of Law, Keith Davey went to work for Foster Hewitt and CKFH radio in sales, rapidly becoming sales manager, a position he would hold for eleven years.

In 1960 Keith Davey ventured into Canadian politics as campaign organizer for his home riding of Eglinton. Having already served as president of Toronto and York's Young Liberal Association, he became the national organizer of the liberal party in 1961. From 1962 to 1984 he was chair or co-chair of eight national Liberal election campaigns. He was given the title 'The Rainmaker' by *Globe and Mail* columnist Scott Young in honour of his ability to precipitate votes for his favourite candidate, like a rainmaker seeding clouds. Senator Davey would later use this title for his political memoir, *The Rainmaker – A Passion for Politics*, which was published in 1986.

In 1966, Keith Davey was appointed to the Senate by Prime Minister Lester B. Pearson. His various contributions these included chairing the important Senate Committee on Mass

Media. He worked closely with Prime Ministers Pearson and Trudeau, offering political advice and sharing warm and loyal friendships.

On his retirement from the Upper House in 1996, his colleagues, under the leadership of Senator Jerry Grafstein, raised funds to honour his contribution to Canada and to political life in this country by establishing a lecture series in his honour at Victoria University. Though Keith Davey retired from the Senate before the required age, he has not left public life and is still active in politics and in his commitment as a family man and avid sports fan. He is married to Dorothy Elizabeth Speare, and they have three children, Catherine, Douglas, and Ian, eight grandchildren, and countless friends.